Mel Bay Presents

FUNDAMENTALS
OF MALLET PLAYING

THE IDEAL METHOD BOOK FOR BEGINNING MALLET PLAYERS

BY JOE MARONI

1 2 3 4 5 6 7 8 9 0

Visit us on the Web at www.melbay.com — E-mail us at email@melbay.com

PREFACE

This method book progresses in a step-by-step fashion. The primary emphasis is on the three essential concepts for learning to play a mallet instrument:

- Learning the names of the notes on the music staff
- Learning the value of the notes and how to count them
- Learning where the notes are located on the mallet instrument keyboard

As new notes are introduced on the lines and spaces of the music staff, the note name, note value, method of counting, and location of the note on the mallet instrument is clearly illustrated.

Each of the essential music elements is presented clearly and sequentially. Each presentation is followed by several exercises and original melodies that are specifically designed to develop reading ability, technique, and musicianship. Students will understand and develop each newly learned music concept as they progress from lesson to lesson.

Also included in this method are seven elementary solos written for Marimba, Xylophone, or Vibes. These solos contain all of the newly learned music concepts that were presented throughout the book. The seven solos are ideal for junior high school band tryouts and Solo and Ensemble contest.

FUNDAMENTALS OF MALLET PLAYING

THERE ARE SIX TYPES OF MALLET INSTRUMENTS

BELL LYRA

The Bell Lyra is used exclusively in the marching band. It is the marching band's equivalent to the bells of the orchestra or concert band. The range is two octaves, A to A. The Bell Lyra sounds two octaves higher than written. The Bell Lyra sounds best when played with hard plastic mallets.

CHIMES – TUBULAR BELLS

The Chimes or Tubular Bells have a damper bar operated by a foot pedal. The range is 1-1/2 octaves, C to F. The chimes sound one octave higher than written. The Chimes sound best when played with rawhide hammers.

XYLOPHONE

The Xylophone has rosewood bars and small resonators. The range is from 2-1/2 to 3-1/2 octaves, F to C or C to C. The Xylophone sounds one octave higher than written. The Xylophone sounds best when played with hard rubber mallets.

MARIMBA

The Marimba is the largest mallet instrument with a range of up to five octaves. It has rosewood bars and large resonators. The range is C to C. The Marimba sounds as written. The Marimba sounds best when played with soft cord wrapped mallets.

ORCHESTRA BELLS - GLOCKENSPIEL

The Orchestra Bells or Glockenspiel has metal bars and is usually mounted in a portable case without resonators. The range is 2-1/2 octaves, G to C. The Orchestra Bells sound two octaves higher than written. The Orchestra Bells sound best when played with small brass mallets.

VIBRAPHONE - VIBRAHARP

The Vibraphone or Vibraharp has metal bars and resonators. An electric motor rotates small metal disks under each bar causing a vibrato effect. The range is three octaves, F to F. The Vibes sound as written. The Vibraphone sounds best when played with yarn wrapped mallets.

Wrist Turning Exercise

Rest your arms at your sides, palms facing in, fingers slightly curved, thumb resting on your second finger.

1. *Turn your wrists until your palms are facing back.*
2. *Turn your wrists until your palms are facing in.*

Repeat the above exercise several times.

Bend your elbows bringing your arms up, parallel to the floor, palms facing in.

1. *Turn your wrists until your palms are facing down.*
2. *Turn your wrists until your palms are facing in.*

Repeat the above exercise several times.

Holding the Mallets

Grip each mallet between the first two knuckles of the second finger and the thumb, placing the thumb on the side of the mallet, one fourth of the way up from the end.

Slightly squeeze the mallet with the thumb and second finger. Rest your first finger on the mallet and curve the other two fingers around the mallet.

This grip provides a very important pivot point.

Ready Position

Point both mallets downward; resting the tips on the keyboard, then raise the tips of the mallets one-inch from the keyboard. Hold both mallets at a 45-degree angle, forming a triangle.

Starting Position

Turn the right mallet up with the palm facing in. Keep the left mallet pointing downward with the tip one inch from the keyboard.

Using Your Foot

It is imperative that you tap your foot on every beat to maintain a steady tempo and to measure the note values. Knowing the note values and having a system of counting them is worthwhile only if you can measure the value of every note with your foot.

PRELIMINARIES

The Music Staff

The MUSIC STAFF consists of five LINES and four SPACES.

LINES   SPACES

The Treble Clef Sign

All music for mallet instruments has the TREBLE CLEF SIGN at the beginning of the staff.

On a staff the notes are either on a line or in a space. The LINES and SPACES have letter names.

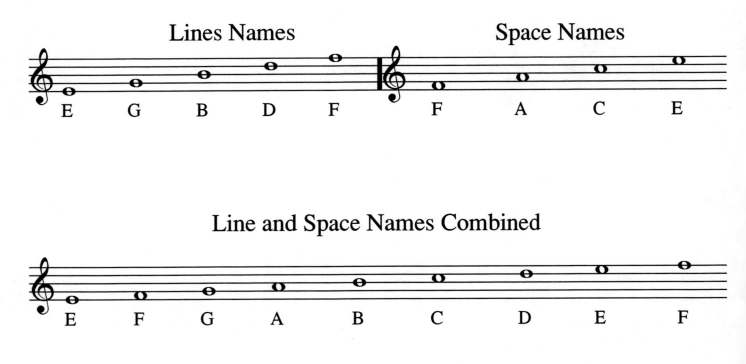

Lines Names
E   G   B   D   F

Space Names
F   A   C   E

Line and Space Names Combined
E   F   G   A   B   C   D   E   F

PRELIMINARIES

Measures and Barlines

BARLINES divide the STAFF into MEASURES.

Single Barline	Double Barline	Final Barline

Measure	Measure	Measure

A Single Barline marks the end of a measure.

A Double Barline marks the end of a section of music.

A Final Double Barline Marks the end of a music composition.

Notes Represent Musical Sounds

Whole Note	Half Note	Quarter Note	Eighth Note	Sixtheenth Note

Eighth Notes are often grouped in 2s. Sixteenth Notes are often grouped in 4s.

Rests Represent Silence

Whole Rest	Half Rest	Quarter Rest	Eighth Rest	Sixtheenth Rest

The above notes and rests will be presented individually and in combinations as you progress through this method book.

Time Signatures

A time signature consists of two numbers; one on top of the other.

The top number indicates the number of beats in each measure.

The bottom number indicates the type of note that receives one beat, 4 = Quarter Note.

Count and tap your foot on every beat.

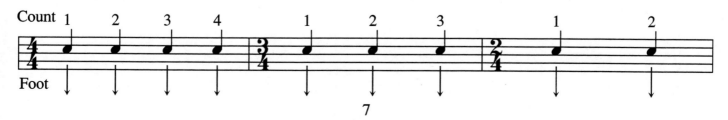

WHOLE NOTES AND WHOLE RESTS

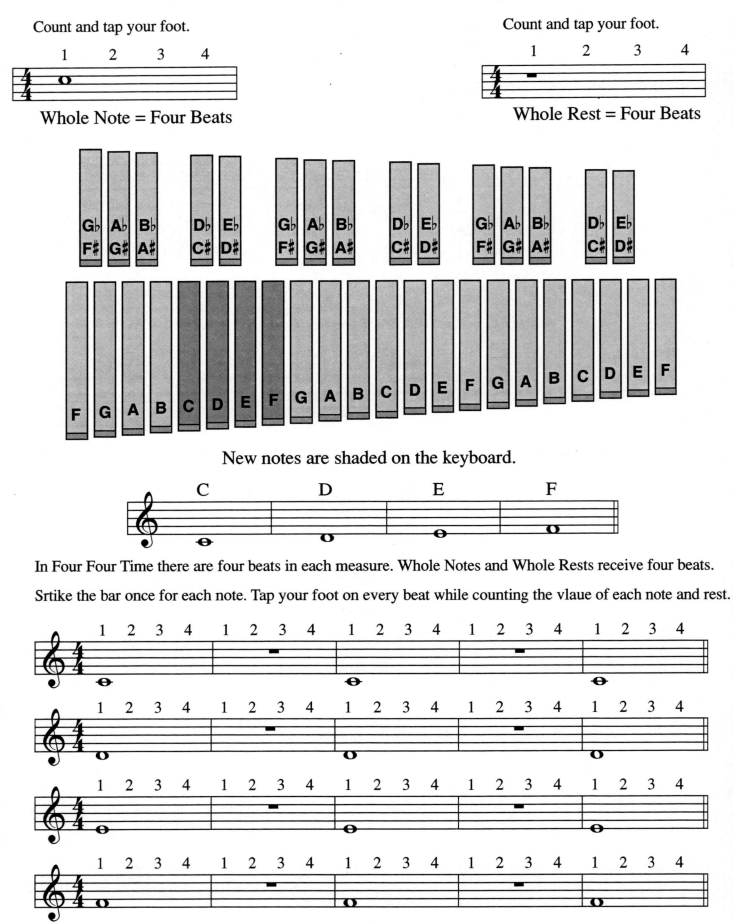

Count and tap your foot.

Whole Note = Four Beats

Count and tap your foot.

Whole Rest = Four Beats

New notes are shaded on the keyboard.

In Four Four Time there are four beats in each measure. Whole Notes and Whole Rests receive four beats.

Srtike the bar once for each note. Tap your foot on every beat while counting the vlaue of each note and rest.

HALF NOTES AND HALF RESTS

Count and tap your foot.

    1   2   3   4

Half Note = Two Beats

Count and tap your foot.

    1   2   3   4

Half Rest = Two Beats

New notes are shaded on the keyboard.

C   D   E   F

In Four Four Time there are four beats in each measure. Half Notes and Half Rests receive two beats.

Srtike the bar once for each note. Tap your foot on every beat while counting the vlaue of each note and rest.

9

QUARTER NOTES AND QUARTER RESTS

Count and tap your foot.

Count and tap your foot.

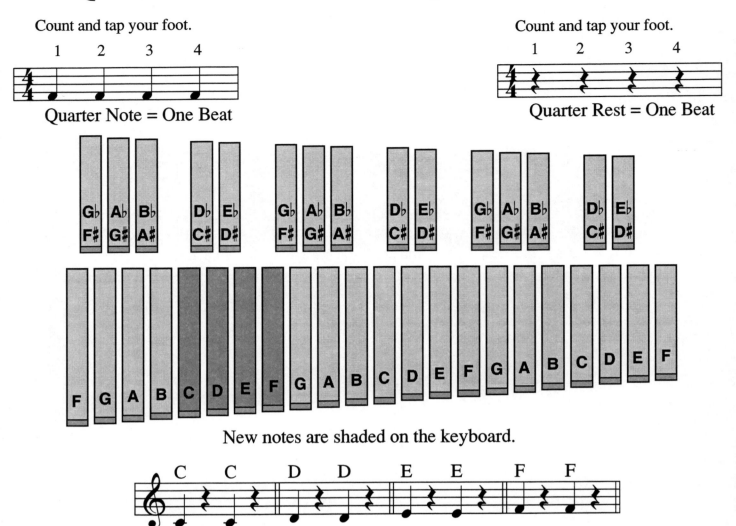

New notes are shaded on the keyboard.

Quarter Note = One Beat

Quarter Rest = One Beat

In Four Four Time there are four beats in each measure. Quarter Notes and Quarter Rests receive one beat.

Srtike the bar once for each note. Tap your foot on every beat while counting the vlaue of each note and rest.

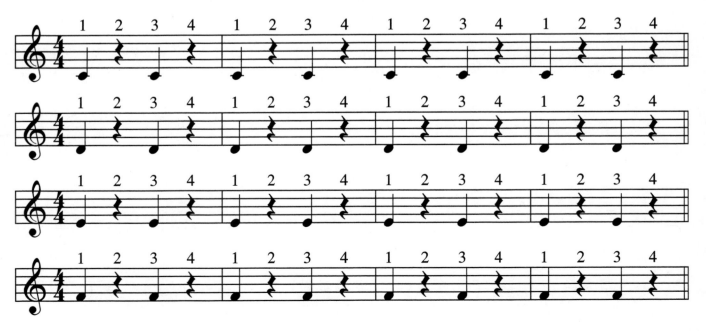

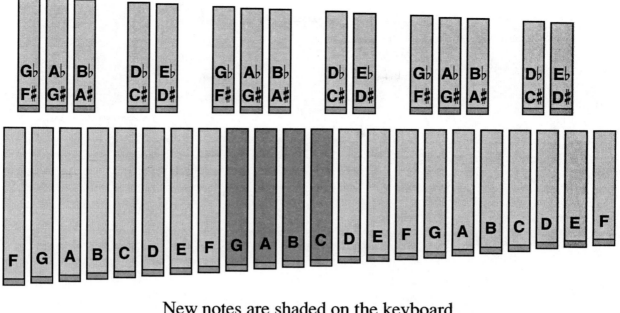

New notes are shaded on the keyboard.

Half Notes and Quarter Notes are always stemmed. For notes on the middle line and above, the stem is down. For notes below the middle line, the stem is up.

Before you begin to play any song, look at the time signature.

MELODY TIME

C MAJOR SCALE

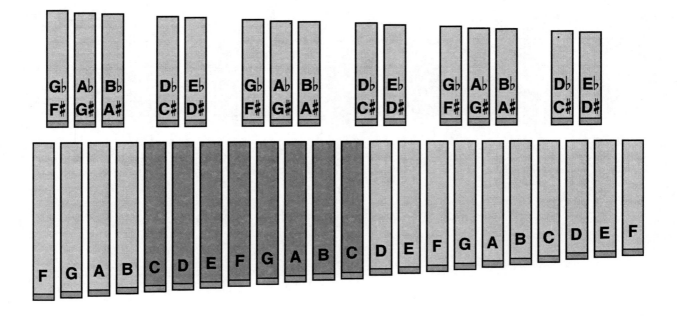

Whole Notes = Four beats

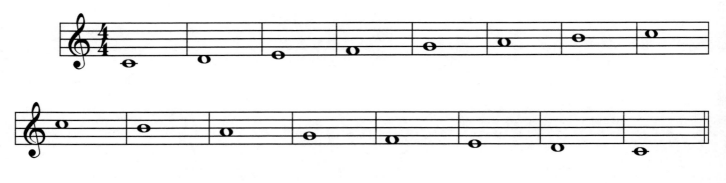

Half Notes = Two beats

Quarter Notes = One beat

MELODY IN C

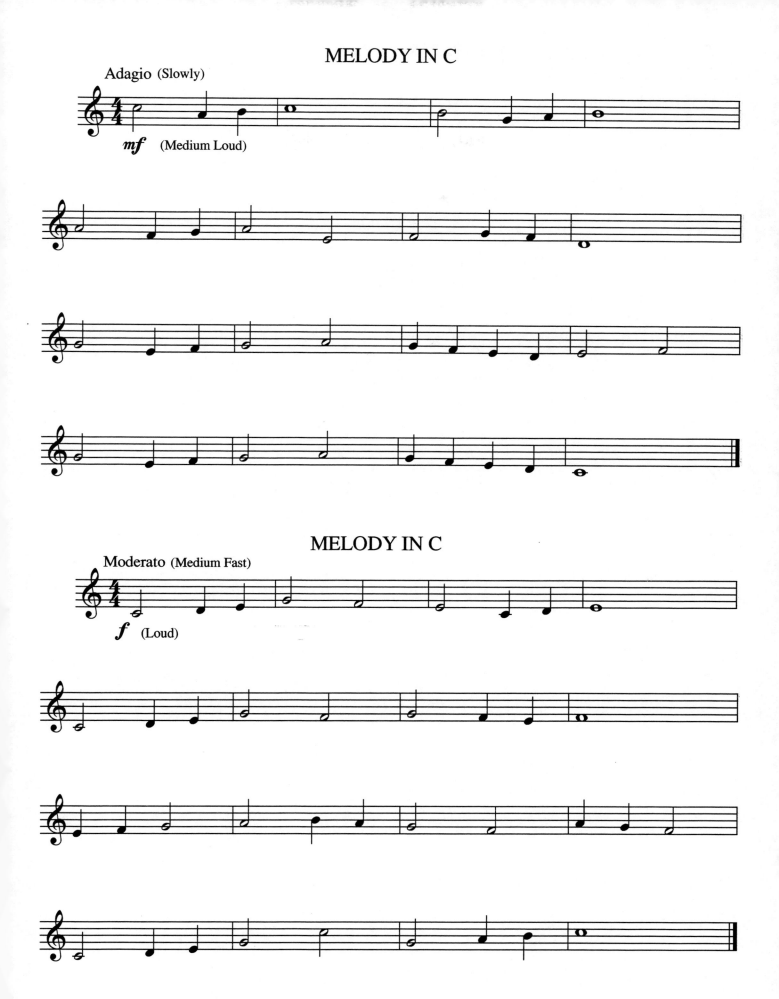

MELODY IN C

THREE-FOUR TIME AND DOTTED HALF NOTES

In Three-Four Time there are three beats in each measure. The Quarter Note receives one beat.

A dot placed after a note increases the value of the note by 1/2.

A Half Note (♩) = two beats, the Dot (.) = 1 beat, the Dotted Half Note (♩.) = three beats.

MELODY IN C

14

CHROMATIC SCALE

Chromatic Scales make use of the Sharp and Flat keys .

A Sharp ♯ is used to raise the pitch of a note - such as F to F♯.

A Flat ♭ is used to lower the pitch of a note - such as B to B♭.

A natural ♮ is used to cancel a Sharp or Flat.

Enharmonics are notes that sound the same but are written differently - such as C♯ and D♭.

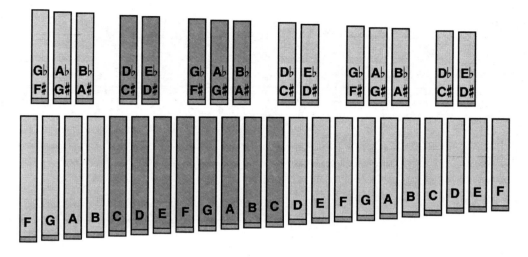

In general, use **Sharps (♯)** when going up the scale, use **Flats (♭)** when going down the scale.

CHROMATIC MELODY

CHROMATIC MELODY

16

ACCIDENTALS

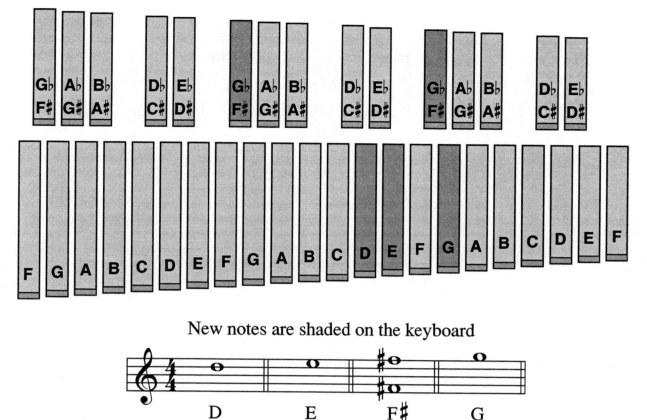

New notes are shaded on the keyboard

Accidentals such as **Flats** (♭) or **Sharps** (♯) are used to temporarily change the pitch of a note.

MELODY TIME

G MAJOR SCALE - KEY SIGNATURES

The G Major Scale has one Sharp which is F#.

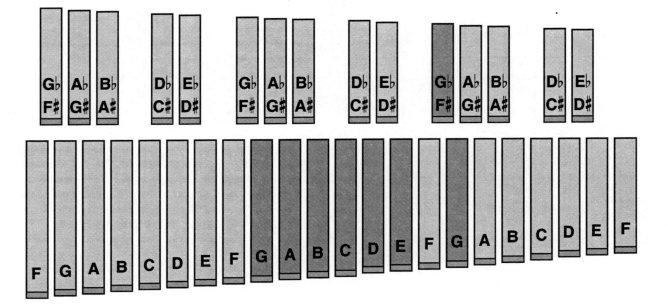

A key signature at the beginning of each staff indicates the Sharps or Flats to be played in that key.

* Remember to play F# in the key of G.

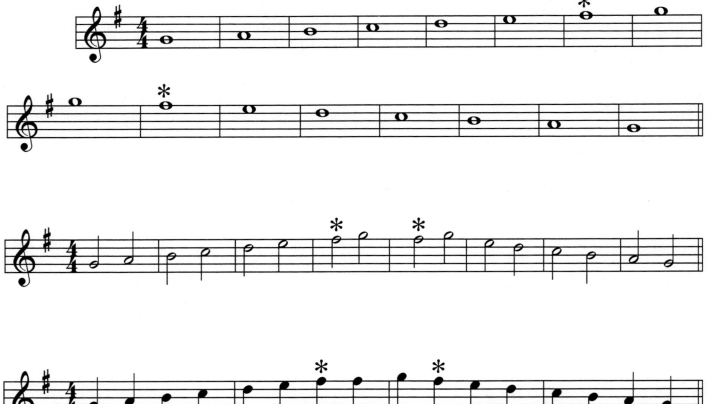

Before you begin to play any song, look at the time signature and the key signature.

MELODY IN G

Two dots before a Double or Final Barline
indicate to repeat from the beginning.

MELODY IN G

COMMON TIME

Common Time is exactly the same as Four-Four Time. The **C** Symbol is used instead of the $\frac{4}{4}$ symbol.

MELODY IN G

LOW NOTES ON LEDGER LINES

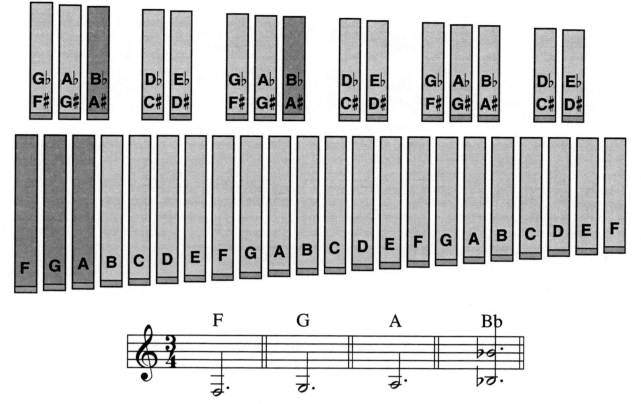

Ledger lines are short lines added below the staff for notes that are too low to be placed on the staff.

Accidentals such as **Flats** (♭) or **Sharps** (♯) are used to temporarily change the pitch of a note.

MELODY TIME

F MAJOR SCALE

The F Major Scale has one Flat which is B♭.

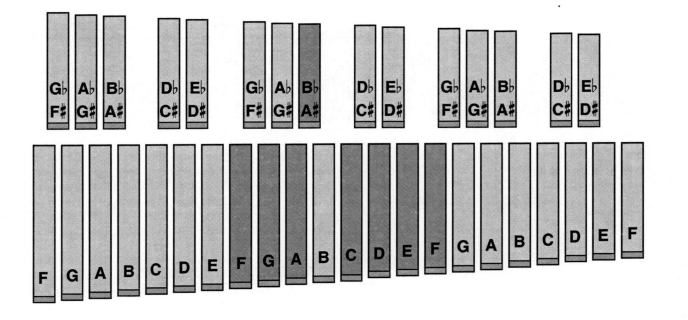

* Remember to play B♭ in the key of F.

22

Before you begin to play any song, look at the time signature and the key signature.

MELODY IN F

MELODY IN F

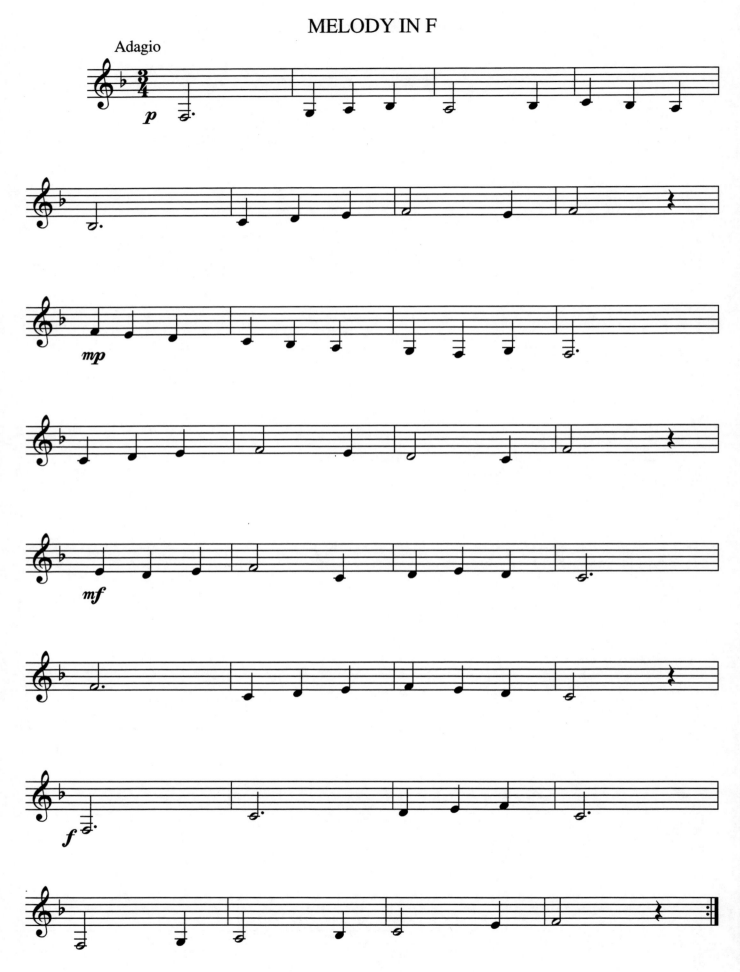

EIGHTH NOTES

An Eighth Note (♪) receives 1/2 of a beat.

Play two eighth notes in one beat.
The (+) means (and).

EIGHTH NOTE EXERCISES

Count and tap your foot.

26

HIGH NOTES ON LEDGER LINES

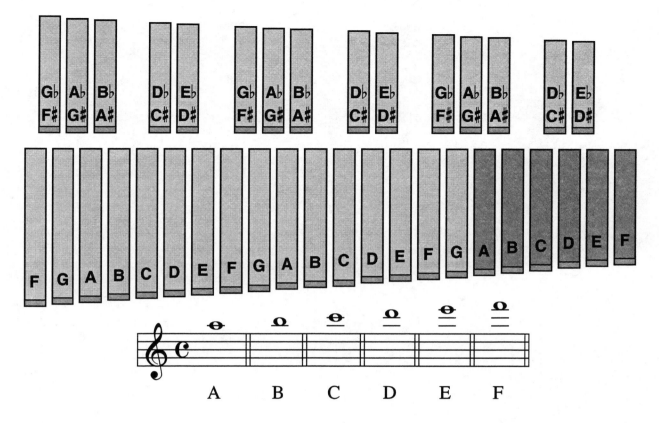

Ledger lines are short lines added above the staff for notes that are too high to be placed on the staff.

MELODY TIME

B♭ MAJOR SCALE

The B♭ Major Scale has two flats which are B♭ and E♭.

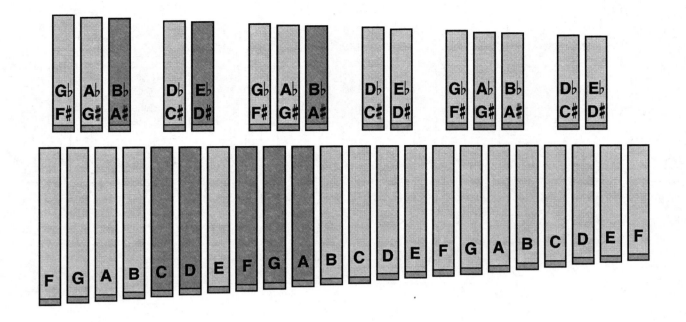

* Remember to play B♭ and E♭ in the key of B♭.

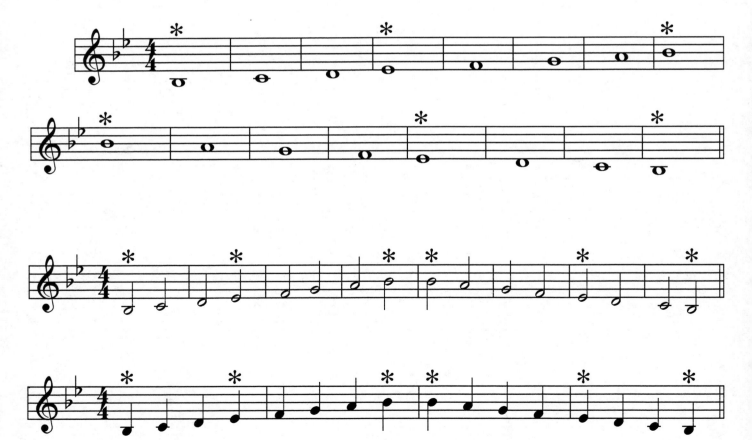

Before you begin to play any song, look at the time signature and the key signature.

MELODY IN B♭

29

TWO-FOUR TIME

In Two-Four Time there are two beats in each measure. The Quarter Note receives one beat.

MELODY IN B♭

(Repeat previous two measures)

(Repeat previous measure)

TIES

A Tie connects two consecutive notes of the same pitch.

Do not strike the second note. Play both notes as one continuous sound.

TIE EXERCISES

DOTTED QUARTER NOTES

A dot placed after a note increases the value of the note by 1/2.

Give the Dotted Quarter Note two beats, then play the following eighth note on the "and" of the next beat.

33

DOTTED QUARTER NOTE EXERCISES

1st AND 2nd ENDINGS

MELODY IN F

(Play the first ending; repeat from the beginning then skip the first ending and play the second ending.)

MELODY IN G

D MAJOR SCALE

The D Major Scale has two Sharps which are F♯ and C♯.

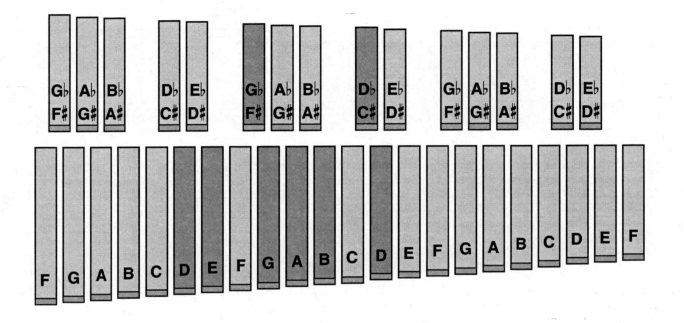

* Remember to play F♯ and C♯ in the key of D.

36

Before you begin to play any song, look at the time signature and the key signature.

MELODY IN D

MELODY IN D

37

MELODY IN D

MELODY IN F

MELODY IN G

SIXTEENTH NOTES

Repeat each line several times. Make sure you count and tap your foot.

40

SIXTEENTH NOTE EXERCISES

MELODY IN C

Moderato

MELODY IN G

Moderato

MELODY IN B♭

MELODY IN F

E♭ MAJOR SCALE

The E♭ Major Scale has three Flats which are B♭, E♭, and A♭.

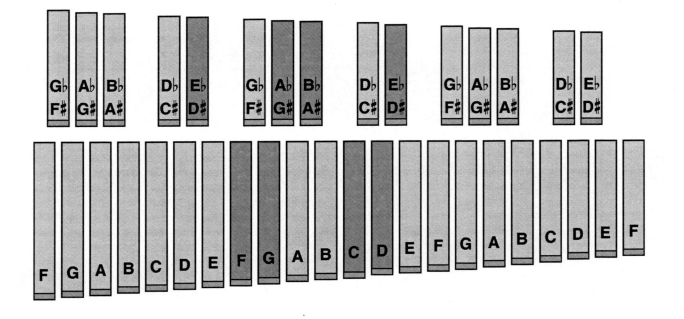

* Remember to play B♭, E♭, and A♭ in the key of E♭.

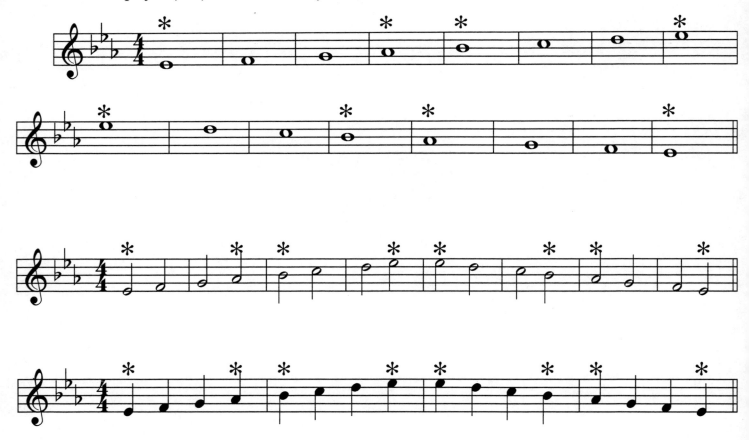

44

Before you begin to play any song, look at the time signature and the key signature.

MELODY IN E♭

MELODY IN E♭

MELODY IN E♭

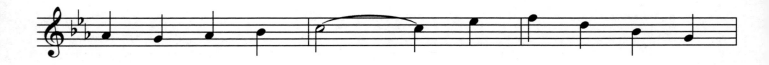

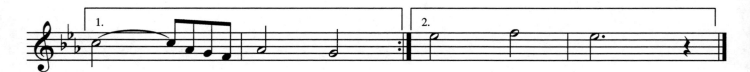

CUT TIME

Cut Time is Four-Four Time cut in half, hence Two-Two Time.

The note values in Cut Time are 1/2 that of Four-Four Time. In Cut Time there are two beats in each measure. Half Notes receive one beat. Whole Notes receive two beats. The ¢ symbol is used for Cut Time.

CUT TIME EXERCISES

MELODY IN CUT TIME

MELODY IN CUT TIME

49

A MAJOR SCALE

The A Major Scale has three Sharps which are F#, C#, and G#.

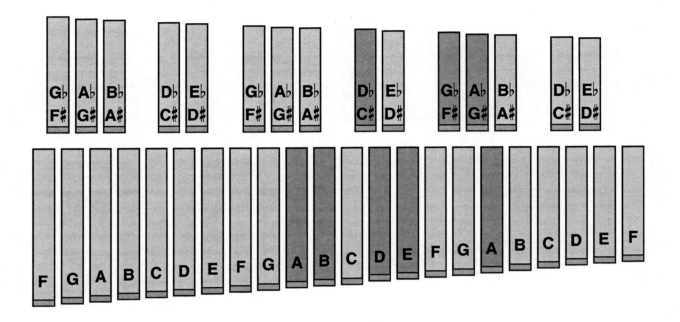

* Remember to play F#, C#, and G# in the key of A.

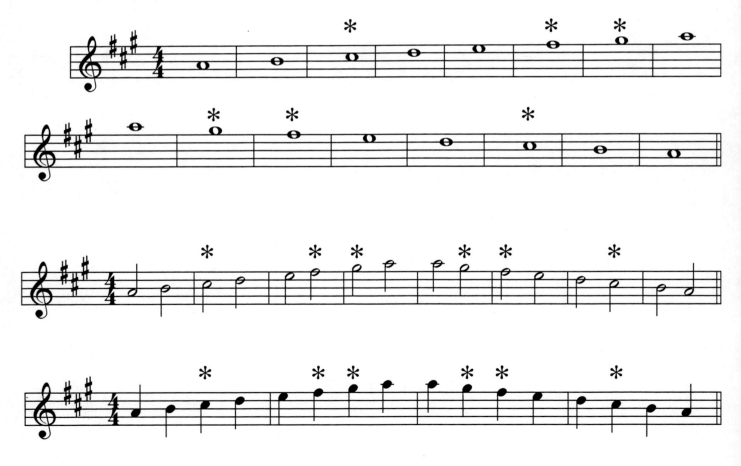

Before you begin to play any song, look at the time signature and the key signature.

MELODY IN A

MELODY IN A

ff _____ *fff* (Very Very Loud)

(Gradually get louder)

MELODY IN A

D.C. al Fine (da capo al fine)

1. Play from the beginning to the D.C. al Fine.
2. At the Double Barline, return to the beginning.
3. Second time, play to the Final Double Barline and end at the Fine.

MALLET MAGIC

D. C. al Coda (da capo al coda)

1. Play from the beginning to the D. C. al Coda.
2. At the Double Barline return to the beginning.
3. Second time, play to the To Coda Sign, jump to the Coda and Finish the song.

LAZY DAZE

D.S. al Fine (dal segno al fine)

1. Play from the beginning to the D. S. al Fine.
2. At the Double Barline, jump back to the Sign. 𝄋
3. Play from the Sign to the Final Double Barline and end at the Fine.

PARADISE

D. S. al Coda (dal segno al Coda)

1. Play from the beggining to the D. S. al Coda.
2. At the Double Barline, jump back to the Sign.
3. Second time, play to the To Coda Sign, jump to the Coda and finish the song.

HAPPY TIMES

LATER ON

GINGER

THE TRAIN RIDE

JOE MARONI

▶ Bachelors Degree in music education with a percussion major
  • Youngstown State University 1967

▶ Masters Degree in secondary administration
  • Youngstown State University 1985

▶ Masters Degree in elementary education
  • Youngstown State University 1991

▶ Teaching private lessons on percussion instruments
  • 40 years

▶ Professional performing musician of percussion instruments
  • 40 years

▶ Percussion clinics
  • Elementary instrumental music teachers

▶ Owner of Neapolitan Music Company
  • Retail music store - 16 years

▶ Retired public school teacher
  • Instrumental music - 31 years

▶ College Professor
  • Youngstown State University 1998 to present
    Computer Science Department

▶ Author of six drum books
  • Published by Mel Bay Publications, Inc.

▶ Author of six percussion ensembles
  • Published by Southern Music Company